Leesa Harker is one of Northern Ireland's best known authors and playwrights. Her three books, *Fifty Shades of Red White and Blue*, *Dirty Dancin in Le Shebeen* and *Maggie's Feg Run* have sold over 33,000 copies; and the stage adaptation of *Fifty Shades of Red White and Blue* (known outside Northern Ireland as *51 Shades of Maggie*) has played to sell-out audiences across the UK and Ireland. Follow Leesa on Twitter, @LeesaHarker, or visit her website, www.leesaharker.com.

Leesa Harker

BLACKSTAFF PRESS
BELFAST

First published in 2013 by

Blackstaff Press

4D Weavers Court

Linfield Road

Belfast BT12 5GH

with the assistance of the Arts Council of Northern Ireland

Printed and bound by CPI Group UK (Ltd), Croydon, CR0 4YY

A CIP catalogue for this book is available from the British Library

ISBN 978 0 85640 920 2

www.blackstaffpress.com

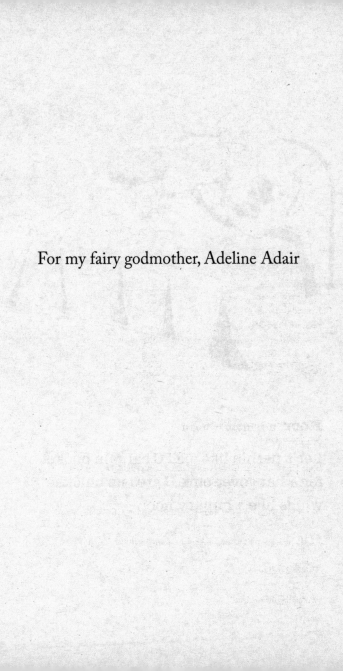

For my fairy godmother, Adeline Adair

Hoor, a wanton woman

Ler's nathin like a KFC bargain bucket for a hangover cure. I ate lem chicken wings like a hungry hoor.

Introduction

Well, sure here bes me til myself ... ya know what we need in lem shaps down le town? A wee book til teach lemens lat don't know hie til spake Norn Iron. An sure ler's nobady better til discuss our lingo lan me. So lis is a wee Norn Iron dictionary – Maggie Muff style! All our wee sayins an slang words are in it – an you'll hear a wee bit about me an le shenanigans lat go on in my world too, til help ye understand it in context anol.

So get yer readin glasses on an a cuppa tea – an maybe a few chums round til read it – an sure le craic'll be ninety (page 32 if ya don't know what lat means).

Maggie Muff xx

Afeared, afraid

Nie one thing I am afeared of is pigeons.
I can't stand lem!

A

Ack, expression of love; or dismay

1) Big Sally-Ann gat wired on Buckey last night an telled me she loved me like a sister. Ack. 2) Len she puked on my new red satin leggings, here's me, 'Ack! See you, wee doll ...'

Affronted, feeling deliberately insulted

I gat telled at le Bru le other day I had til go an work in le pound shap – but when I turned up le boss woulden let me in in case I nicked anything. Cheek! I was affronted! Len I realised I could go back on le Bru – result!

Ampt I, aren't I

I says til Billy, 'Ampt I nat a big ride wih my new hair extensions in?' He said he'd a semi an I was delighted.

Ano, I know

Lis is Big Sally-Ann: 'It's one a'clack –
last orders at le bar, chum.'
Lis is me back, 'Ano – I'm getting my
purse out!'

Anol, and all

Last night me an Big Sally-Ann went
down le town til Rabinsons til buck
some fresh meat. Dolled up til le nines
we were. Fur coats an no knickers anol.
Geg.

Awantin, wanted

Big Sally-Ann's ma used til have til
near throw me out of ler house when
I was a kid. My ma would ring an give
off lat I'd abandoned her. Len Big Sally-
Ann's ma would come an say til me,
'Maggie, love, you may go on down
home. Yer awantin.'

Away in le head, crazy

My ma tells everybady she won Miss
Picky Pool in Bangor in 1985 but
like she's away in le head. She was in
Armagh Women's Prison at le time for
hijacking a milk float.

Away on, you must be joking

I gat a bax of duck in hoisin sauce
in Iceland for me an Big Sally-Ann,
but when I gat til le till it was £4.95.
Here's me til le wee fella at le checkout,
'Whaaa? Away on wih ye, I'll stick til
smiley faces an nuggets, chum.'

Awye, an emphatic yes

Big Sally-Ann telled me she bucked her
second cousin's stepbrother last week.
Here's me, 'Whaaa?'
Lis is her, 'Awye.'
Here's me, 'Whaaa?'
Iss is her, 'Awye.'
You catch my drift.

Backa beyond, far away, the middle of nowhere

Big Sally-Ann an me gat offered jobs down at thon chicken factory in Portydown. Here bes me til le Bru, 'Here, I'm nat traipsing away down ler til pluck a strangled chicken, chum – it's le backa beyond!'

B

Backie, a lift on the back of a bike

Big Billy Scriven was never off a bike
when he was a kid. He was chasin me
even len. 'Here, Maggie, mon I'll give ye
a backie down til le swings.' Here's me,
'Fackaway aff!'

Bake, face

1) When Big Sally-Ann nicked a roll of
scratch cards outta le 24-hour garage
an nat one of lem was a winner, her bake
was pure trippin her. 2) Nelly Lemon
outta le chippy on le Road tried til give
me a tray of batter bits when I asked for
well done scallops. Here bes me til her,
'Nelly, I'm nat lat pissed love. Fill lat
tray wih scallops nie, or I'll slap le bake
clean aff ye, right?' Cont.

Baldy notion, idea, clue, almost always used with negative

My ma has kippers an gin for breakfast. Hie does she nat boke rings round her? I haven't a baldy notion!

Ballbeg, a man's testicles; an idiot; a big dope

1) Big Sally-Ann an Bananaman had a big fall out last week after he telled her she could do wih goin down a dress size. Here bes her til him, 'Fackaway aff, ya big bendy-dicked ballbeg – I'm nat atein lettuce for nobady, right?' 2) Big Sally-Ann starts gurnin at le film *Titanic* as soon as Leo grabs thon piece of wood lat's floatin in le ocean. Like she's seen it ten dozen times, but she still cries buckets. Here bes me til her, 'Here's a hanky – it's only a film, ya ballbeg.'

Ballix; Bollocks;

Ballix, a man's testicles; rubbish (Pronunciation note: Elongating the sound of the word gives utmost effect, i.e. baaaaaaa-lllliiiiiiixxxxxxx.)

1) But, it isn't just for a man's nads. It can be used for women too. Sure I was down at le offie le other week an ler was only one battle a Buckey left on le shelf. Some wee hoorbeg put her hand on it when she saw me goin for it an here bes me, 'Step away from lat battle or I swear I'll bate yer ballix in.' She legged it. 2) Wee Bible-basher Belinda from Agnes Street went on a mission trip til Spain – came back wih a bump. Telled us lat it was an 'immaculate conception' – here bes me an Big Sally-Ann tilgether: 'Ballix.'

Baltic, freezing cold

Le minute ya set futt off le plane comin home from a feg run, ya feel le chill of Norn Iron. Pure baltic. An lat's in July.

Banjaxed, wrecked, useless

Sure Big Billy Scriven gat his schlong caught in his zip when I was givin him a blowie out le back of le kebab shap. I tried til release it but sure we ended up in le Mater: it was sliced til bits like a doner from le shap. Coulden get a good seein til for thee weeks – his dick was banjaxed.

Banter, friendly abuse

Like Billy telled me one day I didn't have til wear short skirts til luck buckable. Nen I says til him, 'What le fuck do you know about style? Yer standin ler like ye've been trailed through a hedge backwards, yaconche!' It was all banter, like.

Bap, a bread roll; head or mind; breasts

1) Le best hangover cure in le world is a well done crusty bap filled wih Tatey

cheese an onion. 2) Our Will says he was gonna join lem Harry Chrishnias. Til move away from Orangeism anol. Here's me, 'You wanna stand outside Primark ringin bells at millbegs an hoods? Wise le bap chum, stick til le Sash.' 3) I was down le Bru last week an some wee new tart had started an was tryin til get everybady a job anol. She tuck a likin til me an wanted til get me intil an old people's home til make lem tea an clean their holes anol. So, here's me, 'Can't work wih old people love – ley give me le horn!' An I flashed my baps at her. Gat barred from le Bru for a week. Result!

Basketti, spaghetti

Big Sally-Ann's ma is a beezer cook like. I'll never forget le first time she made me basketti balls-an-eggs. It was pure gorgeous.

Bate, beat

1) Thelma le hermaphrodite was in le bogs gurnin last week cos some berk telled her lat ley'd bate her good-luckin. 2) Battle a Buckey, Columbo an pastie baps on a Friday night – ya coulden bate it wih a big stick, like.

Beak, play truant

Like me an Big Sally-Ann loved school – for torturing le teachers anol. But at least once a week, we'd beak off, get sausage rolls from O'Hara's bakery, an sit in Woodvale Park all day, talkin shite an havin a geg.

Beetroot, blushing a deep red

Nie, I don't take redners easily. But see when Chesney Hawkes winked at me at le Radio 1 roadshow in 1992, I was beetroot.

Beezer, brilliant

Ler was a nineties rave on in le Shebeen last Sunday night. Me an Big Sally-Ann gat le neon gear on an headed up wih our glowsticks an Vicks anol. We tuck two trips each an danced til le Pradigy for thee hours straight. It was pure beezer.

Belfastian, native of Belfast

After a few days on haliday, ya always get homesick. Len ya hear some wee Belfastian, shoutin in a bar brawl or downin fish bowls of Black Russians an ya think, ack, ler's no place like home, like.

Belter, brilliant

Me an Big Sally-Ann went up til Kellys in Portrush le other weekend til revisit our youth anol at a old skool rave night. Half le Road was ler an I ended

up lumberin a wee spide from Short
Strand. Le craic was pure belter.

Benidorm, a Spanish coastal holiday resort in the
province of Alicante

Le chav capital of Europe an home til le
Queen of Muck, Sticky Vicky. An also,
le tap feg run destination. Ya can't call
yerself a true Belfastian unless ye've
burnt yer baps in Benidorm. I'm tellin
ya, if one of lem planes goes down comin
from Benidorm, ler will be a trillion fegs
splattered all over le runway.

Binlid, idiot

Our Will went down til le Odyssey til try
an get his life-size cardboard cut-out of
Kylie signed by her after her cancert.
Prablam was, it started lashin outta le
heavens an his cardboard Kylie turned
til paper mashee. He was gurnin his
lamps out, le binlid.

Biz, gossip; excited, delighted

1) Wait til you hear le biz! Our Will gat two tickets til le *Nolan Show* an he's give lem til me an Big Sally-Ann! We are gonna go down an start a riot! Yeeeoowwwww! 2) I was walkin down le Road le other day an two wee lawds wolf-whistled me from le other side of le Road. I was all biz. Til I saw lat ley were actually callin ler dog lat was humpin le back of my leg. Friggers.

Blacked, drunk

One battle a peach Cancorde, I'm tipsy. Two, I'm blacked.

Blirt, a woman's front bottom

One of my favourite sleggins is 'I'll hit you a kick in le blirt, ya heg!'

Bog, toilet

I was down in lat new Victoria Centre doin a bidda late-night shapliftin. Ya wanna see le bogs in ler. Swanky – like Buckingham Palace.

Boggin, filthy

Big Sally-Ann's ma is like a clean-a-halic. Here bes her, 'Lat Dora next door is a dirty blirt. She's never done brushin her front step. But you wanna see le washin hangin on her line out le back! Le towels an knickers are boggin!'

Boke, vomit

Have ya seen lat *Embarrassin Badies* on le TV? I was atein a battered sausage le other day when Big Sally-Ann turned it on. Some auld lawd had his nob out til show hie he gat dick-rot off a hooker in Amsterdam. I flung lat battered sausage in le bin an boked. Big Sally-Ann ate

it later lat night in a sandwich, like.
Double boke.

Boogaloo, crazy

Big Sally-Ann's ma went boogaloo when
she found out Big Sally-Ann's da had
pawned her eternity ring til go an see
Rangers at Linfield.

Bout ye, how about you, how are you

It's le best way til say 'hiya' in Norn
Iron. Like, if I'd have met Obama or le
Queen on ler visits, I woulden have said,
'Good morning, and how do you do?'
I'd have said, 'Bout ye, chum? What's
happenin?'

Braven, really

Big Sally-Ann lifted le front of wee
Johnny le mechanic's car when it fell on
him. Like she's braven strong, like.

Bru, Jobs and Benefits Office; money received from the state while out of work

1) Le Bru – where I spend my mornin once a week. It is le mankiest hole in Belfast. Sticky carpets, staff suckin lemons an ya have til sell yer soul for a crisis loan. Plus it's where I met yer man – awye, I near gat my wab knacked in by a ballbeg wih a serious case of le whips an chains about him! Mr Red White an Blue. 2) Nathin like saunterin up le Road til le Shebeen wih my Bru in my back packet. Livin le dream, whaaa?

Buck, have sex

I've lost count of le wee lawds I've bucked. An I've done it every place ya can imagine. In a skip, out le back of le Shebeen, back of a bus, on le roof of Shankill Leisure Centre – le lat. Get it intil ye!

Buck eejit, idiot

No, idiot's just eejit. A buck eejit has til have done somethin praper stupid. Like lat time Big Sally-Ann gat her hand stuck in le teddy bear machine at le Odyssey. Sure ley had til get le fire brigade over til get her arm outta le wee metal hatch thing. Here bes her, 'I spent eleven quid tryin til win a rainbow Care Bear! It's fixed, yez bastards!' Here bes me, 'Sure you've every kinda Care Bear stuffed under your bed, chum.' Here bes her, 'Ano, but I wanted one for you, Maggot.' Here's me, 'You are a buck eejit, wee girl!'

Buckalicious, gorgeous, sexy

Like buckable an delicious mixed tilgether. Ya have til say it while lickin yer lips for full effect. Like see thon Peter Andre an his tan chest an gelled hair anol – I'd wreck thon. He is one buckalicious bastardo!

Buckey, Buckfast wine

Oh, le Buckfast wine, it's so fine. Tastes like a mix of cough medicine an tar – but it gets ya poleaxed in about ten minutes. Fact.

Buckey-ar-la, a cocktail made up of mysterious ingredients

A cacktail lat has secret ingredients lat only me, Big Sally-Ann an Will know. Sure, mon up some time an I'll make ye one, whaaa?

Buckasaurus Rex, a gorgeous man

Thon Chesney Hawkes is getting better wih age. Blonde lacks, sexy smile – he's a big Buckasaurus Rex!

Buggerballs, an expression of frustration, annoyance or disappointment

Ack buggerballs, lis is le last B word in my wee dictionary. Ack.

C

Call, right

Le Bru's no call tellin us we've til clean toilets for a tenner extra a week. Sadists.

Camere, come here

Met lis big sexy American on a feg run til Benidorm. Ya called him Reever. Here bes me, 'Camere Reever, show us yer corndog, big lawd!'

Capshap, police station

Like I think our peelers have a lat til deal wih bein peelers in Norn Iron. Big Sally-Ann's ma always takes a couple a baxes of buns intil le local capshap on Christmas mornin anol. God bless her, like ya could use lem til knack somebady out in le riots.

Catch yerself on, wise up

Myrtle le barmaid at le Shebeen tried til charge us full price for some Slovakian vadki she gat lat fell off a lorry. It was called Modka. Here bes me, 'Catch yerself on, love – we didn't come up le Lagan in a bubble ya know!' Gat it for a quid a shat. Blootered!

Caught short, having an urgent need to go to the toilet

I'll never forget le time Big Sally-Ann was caught short at Zumba after atein a beef chow mein lat was in le fridge a week. She ended up wih her leotard cemented til her arse cos we coulden get it off. Skunderballs!

Cert, a sure thing

Big Sally-Ann drapped Igor after she caught him doggin on le waste ground in le estate. Here bes me, 'Forget Igor. Get up lat Shebeen le night an lumber le bake off le first man lat stands in front a ye! Ya pure cert ye!'

Champ, mashed potato with spring onions

Eh, we call lem scallions, right? Champ's like my second favourite dinner after pastie baps. Wih a dollop a butter on tap. Slabbers are trippin me thinkin about it!

Chinkers, Chinese food, bought from a takeaway restaurant

Nie lat's nat racist! It's just short for Chinese. A chinkers on a Sunday night is just le tanic til put yer hangover til bed. Amazeballs.

Chinwag, chat

Ler's nathin I love more lan me, Big Sally-Ann an Will havin a praper chinwag about our boys over a pat a tea an a couple of gravy rings.

Chum, friend

Like I always start a serious conversation wih le word 'chum'. Like, chum, lis dictionary is helpin lem ones lat can't talk Belfastian til learn le craft. I might be up for a Noble prize or maybe a Bucker??

Clampet, idiot

It's Booker award, ya clampet! Oh awye. Geg!

Clart, idiot

Nie, don't be thinkin I'm a dosey clart – I gat an A in my GCSE French. Passed le oral exam wih flyin colours! Yeeoowwwwwww.

Clinker, brilliant

When Sinead le Greener fell asleep on my settee thon time, I drew 'CONT' on her head wih my eyeliner an she went home til her ma wih it still on. Pure clinker.

Cont, an insult

Le Belfast version of lat other C word. Like if big Billy tries til lumber me when I'm pished, I say, 'Here you, Scriven – fackaway aff. I'm nat lat drunk, ya crafty cont!'

Coupan, face

Any more of yer nansanse an I'll hit you a dig in le coupan. Right?

Cracker, more than brilliant

Big Frank Carson made lis famous wih 'Lat's a cracker!' An it sure was, Frank. Rest his wee soul.

Craic, good times; fun; informal entertainment

A lack-in at le Shebeen when everybady's on tap form an le craic's ninety like. An I'm tellin ya I've had some craic writing lis wee book like.

Crater, a living being, usually an affectionate term

My first wee pet, Snowy le rabbit, gat struck by thunder in le back yard. When I went out til feed her a lettuce, she was tatey bread, le wee crater.

Cream bun, rhyming slang for nun

Two cream buns on le bus up le Road
le other day. Here bes me, 'Wrong bus!
It's le Falls ye're after – le number ten,
chums.'

Creamed or cream crackered, rhyming
slang for knackered, exhausted

Frig me, I went up le Crumlin Road
Sunday market ler til sell some of me
an Big Sally-Ann's auld ravin gear –
I'm tellin ya, it was a day's work. I was
cream crackered by le end of it.

Cryin buckets, crying or sobbing
uncontrollably; weeping

Me an Big Sally-Ann had a wee funeral
for Snowy when she was kilt thon time.
I was all right, like – sung 'Careless
Whisper' anol. But Big Sally-Ann was in
a state – she was cryin buckets.

Culchie, someone from outside Belfast

Nie, I love le Road, don't get me wrong. But sometimes ya just wanna wee bit of fresh meat, y'know? Me an Big Sally-Ann love a wee trip on a blue bus til find a couple of culchies til buck. Pure beezer.

Cut til le bone, mortified, offended, hurt

I'll never forget le time me an Big Sally-Ann went til Dundonald Rave at le ice-bowl. She drunk ten battles of Mad Dog 20 an gat up le nerve til go up til a wee lawd an ask him for a lumber. Only thing was, it wasn't a wee fella – it was a wee girl! She was cut til le bone. An le wee girl was all cut too. It was lem curtain hair dos in le nineties – it was terrible confusin.

D

Dead on, great; wise up

1) A common reply til 'Whaddabout ye?'
is 'I'm dead on, chum, whaddabout you?'
2) Some wee hood from le estate
knacked my door last Halloween luckin
money. Here bes me, 'Aye, dead on,
chum – you're about twenty!'

Dander, to walk slowly; a stroll

I love a wee dander up le Road on a
Saturday afternoon – ya never know
what or who you'll meet.

Dear, expensive

Have ya ever been down in thon House
of Fraser? Ler's hanbegs lat cost a
thousand pound!?! Here bes me, 'Too
dear in here – see ye!'

Decent spud, a nice person

Like Big Billy Scriven's a pain in le
fanny an he lucks like he's had a dig wih
a lawnmower half le time. But he's a
decent spud, like. Ya canny deny lat.

Deck, to hit

Nie, I'm nat aggressive. But I decked
a bus driver last week for takin off at
ninety miles an hour an makin a wee

granny lat was tryin til get a seat fall flat on her face. Nat on, like.

Dickwad, an unpleasant person; an idiot

My Uncle Marty's got le internet in his flat an he's on lem websites luckin a Thai bride. Like who would wanna come til Belfast til live wih a dickwad for le rest of ler life?

Diddie, breast

Big Sally-Ann an me fell out one time in school. She was sittin in Mr Mowat's computer class all depressed anol. So, I snuck outta class an whacked a diddie up against le glass windee on le door. Mr Mowat near had a cardiac but Big Sally-Ann pished herself laughin. Nen we were chums again.

Dig, fight

Big Lynsey Murphy was lumberin le

bake off Samantha Mason's husband at le Shebeen last week an ley ended up near batein le life outta each other on le dance floor. Ack it was a fair dig, like. But bad craic all le same.

Dirt bird, unhygienic, slovenly woman; sluttish woman

Uncle Marty had a visit from a wee Thai woman lat he met online. She came dolled up til le nines – but only had one set a clothes wih her. An I never saw a pair of knickers on his line le whole week. Pure dirt bird. But here, wee Irene lat lives next door til him said she saw her runnin about le back garden in le nip. An Uncle Marty was chasin her. Double dirt bird!

Disturbia, very disturbing, also a popular Rihanna song.

But here, ya called her Ice Cream, like – lat was her name. I asked her why was she called lat. She started gigglin an Uncle Marty started lickin his lips at her. Here's me, 'Whaaa?' Accordin til le gospel Rihanna, Disturbia, like.

Divvy, idiot

When she left, Uncle Marty was cryin at le airport. Til he gat home an realised lat le wee frigger had swiped his laptap, fake Rolex an two hunderd quid. He's a divvy, like.

Do one, leave immediately

I telled Uncle Marty lat if Ice Cream cantacted him or turned up again, he should tell her til do one. Can't be havin lat like!

Doin a line, going out (almost always followed by 'with'), in the sense of a relationship

Going out, my hole. It means buckin somebady's brains out. Like I was doin

a line wih some wee lawd from Tigers
Bay le other week. But he kept sayin he
wanted til get married soon!?! Here bes
me, 'Chill le beans, son!' Drapped him.
One thing I don't need is a needy man!

Doin le double, claiming unemployment benefit
while working on the side and not informing the jobs
and benefits office; a form of benefit fraud

Fraud! Hah! Geg. Half le Road would
get lifted if it was fraud. Sure ya can't
live on forty quid a week, frig's sake!
Ya have til get what ya can lese days by
doin le double. Like ya can't get a battle
a vadki for under a tenner no more.
An fegs are up til seven quid. Hie are
we supposed til live? Big Billy's le King
of doin le double – sure he's a windee
cleaner, fruit seller an door til door
seller of shite.

Dollop, a large serving, especially of food

Uncle Marty went intil a wild depression

after Ice Cream left him, nickin his
money anol. So I went down til his
flat an whacked a big dollop of real ice
cream intil a bowl for him. Here's me,
'Ya can ate that an it'll nat thieve off ye
chum.' He didn't take it well. Cried intil
his hands.

Donkey's years, a long time

Me an Big Sally-Ann have been chums
for donkey's years. We're more like
sisters nie.

Doofer, doofer-dangle-thingymajig,
a person or thing, the name of which is unknown or
temporarily forgotten

Sittin in my ma's le other day, lis is her,
'Maggie, pass me lat doofer-dangle-
thingymajig, will ye?'
Here's me, 'Whaaa?'
Lis is her, 'Le remote, ya daft bat!'
Oh awye.

Dosed, feeling ill, especially with a cold

Even if I'm dosed, I still make it til le Shebeen on a Saturday night. Ler's always some wee spide walkin about wih a Vicks inhaler lat I can barrow anyhie.

Dotin, becoming forgetful or losing memory as a result of age

Like my ma is pure dotin. She tried til light a feg wih a Stanley knife le other day. Near tuck her pinkie off.

Drippin, very wet, soaking

But nat like rainfall. Sure thon time I first saw Mr Red White an Blue down at le Bru, I was drippin like a water tap.

Dry boke, to retch

Nie I love a battered fish. But ya see when big Sally-Ann takes a notion for a jar a cackles an ates lem wih her hands, I get le dry bokes for about thee hours.

Dry hump, to simulate sex, fully clothed

Like I like a wee night out down le town til Bendy-dicks or somethin. But ley're dead reserved down ler. Le most you'll get is a lumber an a dry hump.

Dry nod, a nod in greeting, but for politeness' sake and without warmth

Ice Cream came back wih Uncle Marty's laptap an a suitcase full a thongs lis time. She 'lost le Rolex'. Aye right. Lucks like she's for stayin. I just give her a dry nod like. Don't trust thon as far as I could fling her.

Dunderin inn, shabby, dilapidated or poorly kept house

Two weeks in, an Uncle Marty's house is like a dunderin inn. Ice Cream's a dirty hallion – won't wash a dish. Ler's gonna be trouble ahead. I can feel it in my water.

Eejit, idiot

Like we never say 'idiot' in Norn Iron.
It's eejit all le way! It's nat a harsh thing
til call somebady. When Big Sally-Ann
does somethin daft like tries til do break
dancin at le Shebeen an near puts le
floor in, I say til her, 'Camere, ya eejit,
an get a pint a Buckey down ye.'

F

Fack off, fack away off, fuck off

Like it's an insult. Like when Big Billy
Scriven tries til slip le hand when we're
standin for 'God Save the Queen' in le
Shebeen at le end of le night, I say til
him, 'Fack away aff, will ye? Have ye no
respect for le Queen, ya divvy?'

Fair dos, fair enough

Le other week Wee Agnes in le corner
shap gave me change for a tenner when
I give her a score. Here bes me, 'Nie,
Agnes, ya know I don't shaft my own – it
was a twenty.' So she give me le extra
tenner when she checked her till later
lat night. Here bes me, 'Fair dos, chum.'

Fair play, well done; credit where credit's due

Thelma le hermaphrodite bucked a big sailor from le Tall Ships when ley were down le docks ler. Ya wanna seen him – he was like Arnie Schwartz-a-negger. Fair play til le big girl, like.

Feg run, a holiday taken with the express purpose of bringing back cigarettes, either for sale or personal consumption

Ya go away til Benidorm wih an empty suitcase, fill it wih fegs len sell lem when ya get home for a prafit! Sorted!

Fegs, cigarettes

Le poor man's diazepam. Nerve settler, friend an after-sex comfort.

Faffin about, messing about

Big Sally-Ann tells me til stap faffin about when we're gettin ready for le Shebeen. It takes me ages gettin on me. I had til smother myself in talcum powder last week til get my yella pvc catsuit on. Tuck ages, like.

Fleece, to defraud or charge excessively

Big Sally-Ann's da gave a tenner til two wee girls lat were goin round collectin money for le poor kids in Timbuktu. Here's me, 'Chum – no such place as Timbuktu. Ya were fleeced!'

Fleg, flag

Wee Rannie Buckfast from my flats had his flegs out in November last year. We all thought he'd lost le plat. Turned out his divorce had come through an le only fleg he had til put out was le red white an blue. Yeeeeoowww, wee Rannie Buckfast! Ledge. End.

Flim, five pounds

My ma's never done strokin me for

money. I'm only in le door wih my Bru an here bes her, 'Give us a flim, Maggie, I'm skint.'

Fluke, a stroke of luck

My ma won le jackpat down at le bingo two weeks in a row. Everybady thought it was a pure fluke. But I knew she was buckin le bingo caller. Any way up, sixty-nine!

Footless, clumsy

Big Sally-Ann's footless, like. Ya wanna see le bruises on her knees – especially after a doggin session wih Big Igor! Yeeeoowwwwwww!

Frig, to have sexual intercourse with; to masturbate; more usually used as an exclamation of surprise or as an insult

1) Wee Sinead le Greener's ma tried til marry her off til some auld lawd in

cordyroy so she'd stap buckin wee lawds all le time. She said he was about fifty! Here's me, 'Frig.' 2) Big Billy tried til sell me a bax of double-ended matches. Here bes me, 'Frig away off, you – ler's bound til be something wrong wih lem.'

Full, very drunk

Me an Big Sally-Ann gatecrashed a weddin party down in le Rex Bar le other week. I ended up lumberin le bake off le groom's brother an Big Sally-Ann gat touched up by his aunt Sadie! She blamed it on bein full, like, but I'm keepin my eye on her!

Foundered, extremely cold

I went down til le Bru for my winter fuel payment. Had til wear my ma's duffel coat anol til pretend I was foundered. Bought a ten-week supply of fake tan wih le proceeds!

G

Galoot, clumsy person

I remember me an Big Sally-Ann playin
in le building site down le Road when
ley were building lem new yuppie flats.
Big Sally-Ann stud on a plank of wood
wih a five-inch nail stickin out of it. Went
right through her futt an her LA Gear
trainers, le big galoot.

Ganche, scoundrel

Big Igor le dogger never puts his hand in
his pocket til buy a round at le Shebeen.
Even though he is minted – somehie.
Nathin but a miserable ganche.

Gaspin, thirsty; in urgent need (of something)

Feg runs are amazeballs. But see after
thee hours on a plane, ye're gaspin for a
feg, like.

Gebbin, gossiping

I overheard two wee hoorbegs gebbin in le toilets of le Shebeen about le size a Big Sally-Ann's hole in her red satin leggins. Head-butted le two of lem. Conts.

Geg, a laugh, a good time

Le Shebeen. Midnight. Saturday. Buckey flowin. Tunes on. 'Castles in le Sky' anol lat. Ya can guarantee a pure geg.

Get, contemptible person

Wee Ernie from Agnes Street is a right get. He set up a stall sellin Lady Di memorabilia on le Road le mornin after she died. Wee grannies were buyin scarves lat he swore she'd wore, an teacups lat she'd drunk out of anol. Said le prafits were goin til charity but ley went straight intil le till of le Rex Bar lat night.

Get it intil ye, (literally) get it into you, but more often used to mean go for it

Big Sally-Ann an me were lumberin le bakes off two Russians down at le Tall Ships lat time ley were here. We both came up for air at le same time. Here bes us til each other, 'Get it intil ye!'

Get it outta ye, (literally) get it out of you, but more often used to mean go for it

Big Sally-Ann went buck daft down at le Bru when ley told her she had to do work experience in KFC. Sure she coulden concentrate wih le smell of fried chicken anol. She told le wee girl she was gonna ram a chicken drumstick up her jam roll. Here bes me, 'Get it outta ye big girl!'

Get off ye, take your clothes off

Big Billy Scriven was luckin a sympathy buck le other week cos he lost his winnins from le bookies down a drain in

North Sreet. Like I knew he was talkin
dung, but I decided til humour him,
'Right, will. Get off ye then.'

Get on ye, put your clothes on

Len afterwards he asked if I wanted til
have a duvet day wih him. Here bes me,
'Get on ye, an fackaway aff.'

Ginny-Ann, a scaredy cat, a wimp

Big Billy brought me down a battle a
Buckey, twenty fegs an a Mars bar on
Valentine's Day, God love him. Len he
pulled out a DVD – *Love Ackally* – an
here bes me, 'Fackaway aff, ya big
Ginny-Ann. *Dacter Who*'s on le night!'

Girls' Madal, Girls' Model School

Like le St Trinian's of Norn Iron. Beezer
wee school, like – we gat away wih
murder. Ya didn't do any madellin, like.
Unless ya counted le time we run down

le carridor in our bras an knickers past
Mr Lamont's French class til see if he
gat a semi.

Give it stacks, to put extreme effort or energy
into something

Me an Big Sally-Ann's favourite tune at
le Shebeen is 'You're a Superstar' – we
give it stacks on le dance floor til lat
wee tune.

Give my head peace, leave me alone, stop
making a racket, also a popular Belfast sitcom in the
late nineties

My ma used til go buck daft when I was
recordin le Tap 40 from le radio. Here'd
be her, 'Give my head peace an turn lat
off, will ye?'

Give over, stop it

Big Sally-Ann's da cracked up when
he heard us doin a dance routine til

'Saturday Night' in her bedroom. Here's him, 'Give over, will yez? Yez are near comin through le friggin floor!'

Givis, (literally) give us, but used more often to mean give me

Givis a buck at ye, wee lawd.

Good livin, devout Christian, often teetotal

Ler's a wee good-livin family lives next door til Big Sally-Ann an ya wanna hear le racket of lem singin hymns on a Sunday night. It's worse lan a friggin all-nighter down le estate, frig's sake!

Goin strong, dating seriously, usually for a substantial length of time

Like Big Igor an Big Sally-Ann were goin strong til she found out he was already married til some hoor in Transylvania.

Gorb, greedy person

Like I'm no gorb. But see after a skinful of Buckey, I could ate thee kebabs an a pastie bap for afters. No prablam.

Gormless, lacking intelligence or vitality

It's as well Big Sally-Ann has me. Cos sometimes she's as gormless as ya can get. Big Helen Harbinson, le school bully, had her runnin up an down til le shap at lunchtime til nick her chocolate bars anol. When I found out, I tuck Helen in a Marathon, watched her ate it len telled her it had been ducked intil every bog in le Girls' Madal lat morning. Lat was le last of le trips til le shap!

Granny Mush, a young person who acts older

Like I hate kids, but ya wanna see Big Sally-Ann's cousin's wee girl, Lexi. She's thee goin on forty. She even says 'Here's me whaaa?' A wee granny mush, like.

Gravy ring, a ring doughnut

A cuppa tea, a feg an a gravy ring from O'Hara's on le Shankill was me an Big Sally-Ann's breakfast for donkey's years. Til O'Hara's shut down. It was a sad day, I tell ye.

Grub, food

When I joined thon Slimmin World ley told me I could ate all le grub I wanted – except no pastie baps or kebabs nor nathin! Here bes me, 'Naaaah.'

Gub, mouth

Nen I run down til Beattie's chippy an shoved a pastie bap wih onions an red sauce intil my gub.

Guddies, light trainers with rubber soles, plimsolls

Ya wanna see le hack of le eejits par-walkin up an down le Road. White guddies, vest taps an mascara anol on.

Get a grip, wee dolls!

Guff, ridiculous talk

Big Sally-Ann's ma cracked up at us
when we wrecked her kitchen tryin til
make Buckey cupcakes. Here bes her,
'Get this mess cleaned up nie – an I don't
want none of your guff!'

Gulder, shout very loudly

Nen her da came in an guldered at us
cos we'd used his pipe til stir le mixture.

Gunk, filth, rubbish

In le end, le cupcakes tasted like
nicotine an shite. What a load of gunk.

Gurn, to cry

I never gurn. Certainly nat in public
anyway. But I did gurn a wee bit when
Lady Di died. An ya can't hold lat
against me.

H

Half-cut, well on the way to being drunk

Like my ma says she hasn't a drink prablam. But she takes gin, kippers an a feg for breakfast an she's half-cut before she even gets her bake washed.

Halfers, half shares

Big Sally-Ann's desperate til win big on le scratch cards – even though I telled her she'd never do it. She spent her dole money on lem in le corner shap an I had til buy her drink in le Shebeen an go halfers on a curry chip an cheese after. Pure eejit.

Half-washed, not clean

Big Thelma's a dirt bird, like. She even rolled intil church for Gretta Grimes' wee child's christenin half-washed luckin.

Hallion, a rough, rowdy, outspoken woman; has a connotation of a woman who is sexually liberated

Well, some might say Maggie Muff's a hallion. An ley'd be right! Yeeooowwww!

Hallion battalion, a group of hallions

Me, Big Sally-Ann, Thelma le hermaphrodite an Sinead – le Shankill Road Hallion Battalion.

Ham shank, rhyming slang for masturbation

Big Billy was on at me for a lumber down in le Rangers Club. Here bes me, 'Ye've two hopes, an one a lem's Bob. Away home for a ham shank instead, ya big galoot.'

Happed up, wrapped up warmly

Even in le snow, ya still have til traipse down til le Bru, all happed up, beggin for yer dole money.

Happy days, brilliant

But when it's praper Baltic ya get a winter fuel payment! Yeeooowwwwww. Ya wanna see le rounds bein bought in le Shebeen when le payments are give out! Happy days.

Hard-luckin ticket, ugly

Sinead tried til palm me off wih her cousin Dermott when he came til visit from Donegal. Ya wanna seen le heck of him – cordyroy thee-piece suit an a granda cap. An aside from lat, he's a hard-luckin ticket. Here's me, 'Naaaaaa.'

Hardly, unlikely

Le wee security guard down at le Bru telled everybady lat was smokin electric fegs til get outside wih lem. Said it was cos ler's still fumes. Here's me, 'Hardly. Nie fack aff.'

Harp-six, to stumble, fall

Wee Ali from le estate went harp-six on
a broken grate an gat thee grand in a
claim for twistin her ankle. Next thing
ya know, ler's forty people sittin in le
Mater sayin ley'd fell down le broken
grate too. Chancers!

Hard up, strapped for cash

Hanast til god, people are lat hard up
for money ley'd fling lemselves down a
broken grate til get a few grand.

Harrished, worried, annoyed

Me an Big Sally-Ann went down til do it,
like, but sure le council had been out an
fixed le grate. I said frig lem like. But Big
Sally-Ann was harrished-luckin le rest
of le day about it.

Haven't a baldy, don't know, haven't a clue

Len apparently some wee lawd from le

estate won five grand on a scratch card from Annie Wright's shap. Big Sally-Ann was rageballs after spendin her Bru in ler tryin til win. It's just as well we hadn't a baldy who he was cos she was ready for wringin his neck.

Head bin, idiot

But le head bin lost it. She run down til le shap an put a wheelie bin through le windee!

Head bombadeer, the boss

Len le head bombadeer, Annie's big son Andy, came out an rugby tackled her til le ground. She quite liked it. Dirty baste!

Head showered, to clear your head

I sauntered on back up home til get my head showered – I wasn't in le mood for a brawl in le street.

Head-le-ball, a crazy person

Turned out Andy, le head-le-ball, bucked
Big Sally-Ann in le storeroom of le shap!
Result!

Heel, the end of a loaf

My ma never ates le heel of a loaf –
she throws it out le front door on til le
road for le pigeons. Nen le pigeons hang
around an scare le shite clean outta
me. Conts.

Heifer, a young cow; often used as an insult, to
mean that someone is fat

Nie, Big Sally-Ann's big-boned anol. But
when wee Greener from le estate called
her a heifer in le Shebeen, I stuck le
head intil le wee shite. Hie dare he!

Hell for leather, as fast as possible

Nen he ran off, hell for leather, gurning
his eyes out.

Here's me, whaaa? say what; OMG

My favourite sayin. Like, it can
mean a whole stack of things. It's an
expression of shack, like when Big
Sally-Ann told me she thought she
was up le duff: here's me, 'Whaa?' An
it can also be for confusion. Like my
ma said one time my da was a big ride
– but she's always claimed that she
doesn't know who my da is. Here's me,
'Whaaa?' Iss is her, 'awye.'

Hoke, to dig around looking for something

I hate tryin til hoke out a pound for a
tralley in Iceland. So, I stole a tralley
instead an just keep it in le house.
Beezer idea.

Hole, bottom, anus

Until lat time it snowed, an le tralley
skidded down le Road at fifty miles an
hour an I ended up on my hole in le
Iceland car park.

Hoop, bottom, anus

Len le wee security guard came til help
me up an grabbed my tit by accident. I
slapped his bake an he ended up on his
hoop too. Was a pure shambles like.

Hoor at a hackey match, looking tarty

Me an Big Sally-Ann went til le fancy
dress night at le Shebeen dressed as
Madonna ... in le 'Like a Virgin' days. Big

Sally-Ann's da tuck one luck at us an here bes him, 'Like a virgin? Like a hoor at a hackey match more like!'

Hoorbeg, a woman who will go with almost anyone

Nie me an Big Sally-Ann love a lumber or a touchy-feely-no-putty-inny on a Saturday night. But see thon Gretta Grimes – she'd buck anybady. An I mean anybady. Hoorbeg.

Horse it intil ye, stuff it into you

Big Sally-Ann always had a full Ulster Fry before school when we were kids. I used til be champin at le bit til get my feg at le back of le school bus while she'd be dippin her tatey bread intil her egg yolk. Here'd be me, 'Horse it intil ye, big girl, I'm gaspin for a feg, like!'

Howl on, hold on

Here'd be her, 'Howl on, Maggot, I've a

pop tart til get for afters.'

Howl yer horses, hold on, don't be in such
a rush

Nen we'd be runnin down le street
screamin for le bus til stap. Lem bus
drivers are sadists – ley love ya til miss
le bus. I'd get on le bus an say, 'Howl yer
horses, will ye?'

Hunkers, to squat down, keeping your feet flat
on the floor

Nen me an Big Sally-Ann would go up le
back, get down on our hunkers an have
a sneaky feg. Beezer.

I

Iss/lis is me, and I said

Like my French teacher Mr Nobbin told me I was a natural at French oral. Iss is me, 'Ya wanna see me doin oral out le back of Dundonald Rave, chum.' Gat detention.

J

Jam roll, literally, a traditional steamed pudding made with jam; rhyming slang for bottom, anus

1) I telled le milkman if he give us out-of-date milk again I would hit him a boot in le jam roll. 2) Len le milkman's wife give me le finger as ley drove off an here's me, 'Up your hole wih a big jam roll, yaconche!'

Jammy, lucky

Like I am a jammy cont. My ma always said, 'Maggie, if you fell in a pile a shite, you'd come out smellin of roses.'

Japped, squirted, splatted

Big Sally-Ann gat her diddies japped when she was fryin bacon in le pan ballik naked. She came down luckin Sudocrem. Here's me, where was your clothes? She said Big Igor likes her til cook for him naked. Here's me, buck a duck.

Jamember, do you remember

Jamember years ago, ya could get a tin of coke, a packet of crisps an a bar of chocolate for a quid? Lem were le days.

Job, criminal act

Ya know shit's goin down when Big Billy Scriven says he's away on a job. He'll either end up sellin TVs up in le Shebeen or lifted an in le capshap.

Job's a goodun, a job done well

But he did get some a lem lady shavers one time an me an Big Sally-Ann gat one for free. Here's me, 'Job's a goodun.' But we gat pissed, shaved our muffs an fell asleep. Big Sally-Ann's cat ate le shaved hair an puked up a pube fur-ball le next mornin. Well, I boked for Belfast, I tell ya.

Jookie, a sneaky look

Like I took a jookie at Big Sally-Ann's muff an she'd done hers intil le shape of a heart for Igor. Ack.

K

Kacks, knickers

See lem PVC leggings – ley're beezer,
like. But ya have til wear no kacks til
get le full effect. Nat a prablam for me,
but Big Sally-Ann still wears her granny
knickers an suspenders underneath
hers an ya can see le lat.

Kack-handed, inept, clumsy

I tried til shape my muff intil a flower.
But sure I'm kack-handed an I ended
up wih a wonky shamrock. Well, it is a
shared future after all.

Kebs, feet

Some wee lawd tuck my shoes off an
started til suck my toes one time an
here's me, 'Holy shit! My kebs smell like
onions an vinegar!'

Keep dick, keep a lookout

Big Sally-Ann's shite at shapliftin, like.
But she's good at keepin dick while I fill
my beg.

Kenn Dodd, rhyming slang for Protestant

I once had a wee fella turn me down for
a lumber cos I was a Ken Dodd. Here's
me, 'Whaaa? Is your head cut? Get your

lips over here nie or I'll send ye back til Ardoyne wih a red hand of Ulster on yer arse.' He saw my point in le end.

Knees done, a paramilitary punishment in which the victim is shot in the kneecaps

I give Big Billy Scriven a sympathy buck lat time he gat his knees done. Len I found out he hadn't been shat, he'd only gat a wee operation til take out a varicose vein! Le wee frigger!

Knickers are ridin me, an extreme wedgie

See by le time I march up til le field every Twelfth, I'm sweatin gravy an my knickers are ridin me. Thank God for pokes an Paisley.

L

Lacin, beating; vomiting

1) When Janny from le Road cheated on
Thelma le hermaphrodite, she give him
a quare lacin out le back of le Shebeen.
2) Big Sally-Ann missed it cos she was
in le bogs lacin rings round her.

Lamp, eye; to hit

1) Janny came in wih a busted nose,
gurnin his lamps out. 2) Nen Thelma
lamped him again for bein a big girl
about it.

Lash, to vomit; to rain

1) Len I run til le bogs an lashed rings
round me too. Here bes me, 'I knew lem
cackles we gat from Kircubbin was a
bad idea!' 2) I love lyin in bed when it's

lashing outside, gettin my back doors smashed in by some big buckasaurus rex. Pure beezer.

Lick an a pramise, a quick clean up, with the promise that you'll do it properly later

My ma wasn't one for mornin routines when I was a kid. I was sent out til school wih a lick an a pramise an a digestive biscuit buttered for my breakfast. Did me no harm like.

Late-night shapliftin, shoplifting in
the evening

I love goin down le town at Christmas
for a bidda late-night shapliftin. All le
wee dolly birds in Debenhams are too
busy luckin at lemselves in le mirras til
catch me shovin a perfume gift set up
my jumper.

Le Road, Shankill Road

Le Road til me is le Shankill, or le heel
an ankle some call it. But le Road is like
le main road where you live. Le Falls
Road, le Shore Road or le Newtownards
Road all get called le Road too.

Lifted, arrested

Jamember thon time Big Sally-Ann
gat lifted an I stood outside le capshap
wih a banner lat said 'Free le Shankill
one!' Geg.

Lig, idiot

An le big lig was busy buckin some wee capper in le cell le whole time! She was rageballs when ley let her out – she wanted til stay in.

Lilty, a light-footed person; a holiday

1) When she finally gat out, she was away like a lilty up le Road til le Shebeen til tell us all about it. 2) Big Sally-Ann's ma an da went away on a lilty le other week til Bundoran. Left me an le big girl til fend for ourselves. We were scunnered. No Sunday dinner – nathin. Big Sally-Ann was for ringin Chile-line anol.

Lit, to go for (someone)

Thelma le hermaphrodite said Big Sally-Ann was talkin balls about buckin le peeler lat time an I lit on her. She was pure jealous of Big Sally-Ann because she was dyin til get buckin a big capper herself

Lock, a lot

We ended up drinkin a lock of Buckey an havin a pure geg lat Big Sally-Ann was released.

Lumber, a long kiss; to kiss

I even lumbered Big Billy Scriven I was lat happy. He was all biz. Cont tuck a video of me goin at him an sent it til everybady on Facebook. I was skundered.

M

Ma, mother

If ya could call her lat. My ma's a bitter oul trout, like.

Maggot, idiot

Aywe – an it's my nickname. But only Big Sally-Ann calls me lat. It's our wee 'thing'. It's dead funny when she says, 'Maggot, stap actin a maggot will ye?' Geg.

Make tracks, leave

When le Shebeen's closing, I always say til Big Sally-Ann, 'Mon chum, let's make tracks.' But sure she's always le last one out, downing everybady's dregs on le way to le door.

Manky, worthless, rotten

Like le Shebeen's a manky hole. But we pure down love lat wee place.

Meat wagon, police car

Ler's always a meat wagon hangin about le estate. My wee granny (God rest her) used til go out wih ten cups a tea an a packet a Nice biscuits for lem in le winter. Wee crater. Was prababy luckin her hole, like. But sure.

Meathead, idiot, usually male, sometimes muscly

That Igor is nathin but a big meathead. He's more muscles than sense. I dunno what Big Sally-Ann sees in him. Oh, wait a minute...

Melt, unspecified body part, almost always preceded by 'I'll knock your ...'.

I telled him, 'See if you ever hurt my mate, I'll knack yer melt in, right?'

Melter, crazy person

Thelma le hermaphrodite's a pure melter. She was doin a line wih my Uncle Marty one time – len Ice Cream found out an went round til sort her out an she ended up doin a line wih her too! Do nat ask.

Ménage-à-thee, a sexual arrangement, usually involving a couple and the lover of one of them

Ice Cream, Thelma le hermaphrodite ... an my Uncle Marty in le middle? Lat's a ménage-à-thee lat I do NAT wanna see. My eyes are bleedin thinkin about it.

Mere, come here

My favourite chat-up line is, 'Mere big lawd! Givis a buck at ye!'

Messages, shopping

Some wee swank from le estate gets her
messages delivered. Can ya believe it?
Delivered. Like I know her fella's made
a money nie he's doin le double – taxiin
on le side. But getting yer messages
delivered? Never heard le likes of it.

Millbeg, Belfast female chav

Nie some people say I'm a millbeg. An I
suppose I am. But I'd rather be a millbeg
lan a swank who gets her messages
delivered.

Milly, originally the nickname for female mill workers, which has now come to mean a female chav

Millbeg comes from milly – lat was
le nickname of women who worked
in le mill years ago. Like my granny
did. Le start of generations of strong,
independent women. So, I'm proud
til be a milly!

Minger, a disgusting person

Big Sally-Ann is a minger sometimes,
like. She tuck a pizza crust outta my bin
one Sunday morning an dipped it intil a
pickle jar. Said it was a hangover cure.
Here's me, 'Yer nat wise chum.'

Mingin, disgusting

My flat's mingin le day. I've had lat
many parties lately – I need til run
up an down wih a magnet til get all le
empty cans lifted an ler's a crust on
my bedsheets. Well, I can't help bein
buckalicious, can I?

Mon, come on

Here bes Big Sally-Ann, 'Mon. Get
le rubber gloves on an we'll clean up
lis shithole.'

Mon will, come on then

I says, 'Sure I tuck lem rubber gloves up
til Big Billy's for a bidda role play. Bare
hands it is, chum. Mon will.'

More power til your elbow, may you have
strength; good on you

My Aunt Adeline was dead proud of me

writin lese wee books anol. Here bes
her til me, 'More power til your elbow,
Maggie!'

Mucker, mate

Like Big Sally-Ann's my best mucker. I
coulden do without her.

Mug, idiot

I'm no mug. When Ice Cream asked til
barrow a fiver from my Bru, I give her
one of my fake ones from le Monopoly
game Big Sally-Ann gat me. Shove a
flake in lat, Ice Cream!

Munter, an unattractive woman

Ice Cream's been learnin our lingo.
When she gat rumbled wih le fake fiver
at le corner shap, she run back down
an shouted up til my windee, 'Maggie
Muff, you a munter!' Here's me, 'Ya can't
stroke a stroker, chum. Nie fackaway aff!'

N

Naff, in bad taste

Uncle Marty went down til Jean Millar's an gat Ice Cream a weddin dress. Ya wanna seen le heck of her – it was peach an pink. It was naff, like.

Nebby, nosey

I'm so nebby, I lucked at le ticket, an it said 'NOT FOR SALE'. Here's me til myself, lem two's done a runner in le sample dress. Thievin shits!

Neck, swallow

But I decided til bury le axe wih Ice Cream, seein she was gonna be part of le family anol. So I give her a Buckey-ar-la an told her til neck it.

Neggin, pestering or annoying

She ended up blacked an started neggin Uncle Marty til get her a praper engagement ring.

Nen, and then

Nen he gets fed up, flings her over his shoulder an walks out le door.

Nie, now

Nie, I'm all for women's rights anol, but thon's a wee firecracker when she starts – I dunno hie he's gonna handle her.

Nip (usually used with 'in the'), naked

I happened til tell Big Billy Scriven I had le hats for Jimmy Nesbitt, le actor, after seein him in le nip wih a rose between his arse cheeks in Cold Feet. Len Billy turned up til my door on Valentine's Day ballik naked an passed me a rose from his arse cheeks. I was nearly flattered ... til I saw le skid mark on le rose.

Nobbin, having sex

I doubt Uncle Marty will be worryin too much about Ice Cream's temper when ley're nobbin on his trusty pink suede sofa.

Norn Iron, Northern Ireland

I pure love Norn Iron. Like we have our wee prablams anol ... but ler's no place I'd rather be.

O

OMG, oh my god

When Big Sally-Ann text me tellin me
she'd bucked a wee lawd under Niagara
Falls lat time she went til Canada til
visit her relatives an I coulden go cos I
gat le mumps by lumberin le bake off a
tramp down le town, all I could text back
was, 'OMG'.

Oddball, strange person

Like Thelma le hermaphrodite's all
right. But she's a bit of an oddball at
times too. Ya coulden call her yer mate
like. She doesn't like getting close to
anybady. Unless she's buckin lem of
course.

Offies, off-licence

Me an Big Sally-Ann's barred from le
offies nie cos I gat caught wih a battle a
Buckey up my sleeve, an Big Sally-Ann
pretended til trip on a floor tile til get a
claim. Miserable conts.

Old Year's Night, New Year's Eve

Le swanks call it New Year's Eve. But til me, it's always Old Year's Night. Say 'see ye' til le year behind ya an when le boats sound ler horns at le dacks in Belfast at midnight, ya think, Happy New Year – bring it on!

Oul, old

'My oul man's a binman, he wears a binman's cap.' Lat's a wee song Big Sally-Ann used til sing when her da done le bins.

Oul doll, old woman

My ma's an oul doll, like. But when she's sober, an gets herself dolled up til go til bingo, she's nat half bad-luckin.

Out on le tear, out for a night on the town, out for a night of fun

Me an Big Sally-Ann's out on le tear le

night! I've my red suspenders on an a packet of three – ribbed for my pleasure – whaaa? Lack up your sons!

Oxters, armpits

Well, I started cleanin le flat. I was up til my oxters in feg butts an Buckey battle taps when le buzzer went. Big Billy wih a pastie bap an my rubber gloves. Here's me, 'Right, you dirty dirty boy – get in lat bedroom nie til I give you a good scrubbin!' An I chased him in ler.

P

Pan, head

My ma used til wake me up as a kid wih, 'Maggie get up nie or I'll be up lem stairs til knack yer pan in before ya can say "Chesney Hawkes"!'

Paralytic, very drunk

Big Sally-Ann gat paralytic at her cousin Alison Akay's wedding til a wee Turkish fella an she ended up dry-humpin his da on le dancefloor at le evenin do til 'Summer Jam'!

Paris bun, rhyming slang for nun

Nie I'm nat a racist, I helped a wee Paris Bun across le Road le other week. She was about ninety, God love her.

Pass myself, to greet someone, but only for politeness sake and without much warmth

Gretta Grimes lied about buckin Big Billy Scriven, an about him being le da of her wean but like I felt sarry for her. So, when I see her nie, I pass myself an carry on.

Pastie, a fried meat and potato patty, a Northern Ireland speciality

Never mind scallop pasta, what big sexy Nigella wants is a pastie bap wih red sauce. She'd love it!

Peeler, police officer

Ice Cream phoned le peelers cos she said Uncle Marty was gonna bate her. But all he said was 'bate that intil ye' when he done her a bacon sandwich! God love her – she still hasn't gat our lingo.

Piece, sandwich

Big Sally-Ann started doin dog walkin for le elderlies down in le estate as part of her community service for putting le shap windee in lat time. I was dead proud of her. I made her favourite piece for her, tuna mayo, an gat her a skatch egg anol. She was all biz.

Picky Willick, someone who picks their nose

Big Sally-Ann's wee nephew Cooper is a picky willick, like – le dirty wee shite.

Piggin, dirty

Big Sally-Ann came back from dog-walkin piggin. Lem dogs hadn't been walked for ages an ley went buck daft jumpin all round her. But she still loved it, like.

Pish stap, a toilet break

We gat le bus up til Kelly's wih our carry outs le other week an stapped for a pish stap on le motorway. All good like. Til Big Sally-Ann gat le Brad Pitts. Skundered.

Poke, ice cream cone

Musta been le poke she gat in le Shebeen le night before. Some dirtbird was sellin

Buckey pokes an she'd about ten of lem.

Poleaxed, very drunk

In le end, we had a beezer night. Gat poleaxed an lumbered le bake off two wee lawds from Glencairn.

Pure, very, extremely

Goes before somethin til tell ye it's extra-special brilliant. Like lis wee Norn Iron dictionary is pure beezer, like.

Q

Quare-luckin ticket, very attractive

Wee Ernie next door til my ma has been after her for years – God knows why. He says til her, 'Mornin, morning, yer a quare-luckin ticket the day!' I near boke.

Quare, very

Me an Big Sally-Ann have been best mates a quare an long time like.

Quim, vagina

Nie I loved kinky sex wih Mr Red White and Blue – like le ice cream bit, nat le whippin bit. But I woulden do it wih mint choc chip again after getting lem choc chips rammed up my quim. Nat nice.

R

Ragin, very angry, furious

I be ragin when I find out I've missed an episode of *Columbo*, like. Even though I have le bax-set an can watch lem any time.

Ram-stam, rush into something

I love le way Columbo ram-stams intil le murder scene wih his bonk-eye an his wee cigar anol. Pure beezer.

Rap, knock

Len he raps le door of le murderer's house an says, 'Eh, one more thing ...' I love him!

Rare bear, an odd or unique person

Like people would say me an Big Sally-

Ann are rare bears, like, cos we love *Columbo* an Chesney Hawkes anol. But like ya can't all be le same. Ley broke le mould when ley made us!

Rare, to bring up

Ya coulden say my ma was a loving mother, like. She was blacked for most of my childhood. Lucky for me Big Sally-Ann's ma rared me good an praper.

Ratten, rotten

Sure my ma used til send me til school rattan. Nen Big Sally-Ann's ma stepped in an bought me a new uniform anol. Love her til bits, like.

Red up, tidy up

I red up my flat once a month – whether it needs it or nat.

Redner, red with embarrassment

Here, I tuck a pure redner le other day. Sure my skirt blew up in front of a load a builders down le Road an I'd my leopard print thong on. But lat wasn't what embarrassed me – I'd bucked some wee lawd from le estate le night before an he'd give me a love bite on my left cheek!

Right one, crafty person

But here, he was a right one. Snuck off early le next mornin an swiped my last battle a Buckey on le way out le door!

Right you be, right you are, okay then

I rung Big Sally-Ann an telled her til come round an we'd dander down til KFC for a cure. Here bes her, 'Right you be, chum, won't be long.'

Rounders, a ball game in which players run between posts after hitting the ball, scoring a rounder if they run around all the posts before the ball is retrieved by a player from the other team

Rounders was me an Big Sally-Ann's favourite thing at school. Except smoking in le toilets, of course.

Rightly, just approaching drunkness, tipsy

Guess who I saw sittin in KFC? Yer man who nicked my Buckey. Here's me 'Bout ye!' He hadn't a clue who I was. He was rightly. Cont.

Rinse, to make a fool of someone

So, I yanked le Buckey an his Bargain Bucket off him an left him sittin wih nathin. Berk gat rinsed, like.

Rubbered, very drunk

One time we sneakied a battle a Buckey intil school an downed it at break time. We were rubbered in Geography!

Runt, sneaky person

Len Helen Harbinson, le wee runt, squealed on us an we gat sent home til dry out. Result!

S

Sanger banger, a girl who goes with soldiers

Me an Big Sally-Ann went through a wee stage of bein sanger bangers, like. Lem English accents an muscles anol had us frothin at le mouth. We love a man in a uniform! Soldiers, peelers, firemen, Salvation Army ... le lat.

Scallop, battered potato slice

A portion of well-done scallops drowned in salt an vinegar, a battle a chilled Buckey an le *Stephen Nolan Show* on TV – perfect Wednesday night in.

Scary biscuits, very scary

Some of lem wee Salvation Army ones are hornballs, like. Scary biscuits!

Scunnered, annoyed

I gat short-changed down in le Spar le other day by a tenner. By le time I realised, it was shut. I was scunnered like.

See ye, literally see you, but more usually used to mean goodbye

Went down le next day til trail le wee cashier an here bes her, 'I never short-changed ye ... see ye!'

Settle yerself, settle petal, calm down

I started gulderin at her – len le wee security guard came over an here's him, 'Settle petal ... I'll see ye right.'

Shebeen, illegal drinking den

My favourite place on le Road. Le security guard ended up takin me up ler an buyin me drink all night! Yeeeoowwww!

Shuck, ditch; crack (of bottom)

Len he chased me down til my flat. I was huffin an puffin an le sweat was runnin down le shuck of my arse.

Sick as a dog, very sick

Le next day, after a skinful of Buckey an a rampant session wih le security guard, I was sick as a dog.

Sicken, to disgust

But it was still annoyin me lat le wee cashier had nicked my tenner. It would sicken ye like.

Sickener, to have had enough

Big Sally-Ann's ma had a sickener of her da spendin his DLA in le bookies. So, she chapped up his wooden leg so he coulden get ler. Bit dramatic like, I thought.

Skelf, splinter

Me an Big Sally-Ann tried til put it back
tilgether for him an I ended up wih a skelf.

Skelp, slap, wallop

Some weans lese days are spoilt brats
– ley need a good skelp on le arse like
you'd a gat in my day!

Skinny mallink, very thin person

Sinead is like a size ten – a skinny
mallink. But I still think a bidda chunk
in yer trunk's more attractive!

Skint Eastwood, broke

I am gonna have til stay in all week til
Saturday night. I'm Skint Eastwood, like.

Skitter, troublesome person

Big Billy Scriven can be a wee skitter,

like. He put Ernie's false teeth in Big Sally-Ann's pint le other week an she gat a mouth fulla somebody's teeth when she took a drink.

Skitters, diarrhoea

Turned her lat much, she had le skitters!

Skittery, crafty

But Big Sally-Ann can be a skittery wee shite too. Til get him back, she emptied an ashtray intil his pint an he ended up wih a mouth fulla feg butts. Yeeoowwwww!

Skivvy, slave

Le Bru thinks all us dolers are skivvys, like. Line up here, sit down ler, fill lis in, sign lat. As if we haven't better things til be doin!

Skrake of dawn, early morning, crack of dawn

An ya have til get up at le skrake of dawn til go an sign on nie. Ya wanna see le bunch of hungover, scraggy, half-pissed eejits walkin down le Road til sign on. It's like le *Dawn of le Dead*.

Skud, curse

Yer woman on le till at le Spar put a skud on herself, like, when she tried til rip me off – lis time she tried til stroke an oul doll of a tenner an le oul doll bate her round le bap wih a battle of cream soda. Karma's a cont, chum. Geg.

Skunder, to embarrass

Nie it takes a lot til skunder me. But lat time I gat caught ballik naked on le beach in Turkey by a wee family from Leeds after a night on le razz ... I was pure skundered, like.

Slabber, to bitch; to drool

1) Nie ler's one rule about best mates: never ever slabber about each other. End of. 2) Ya can smell Big Sally-Ann's ma's Sunday roast from le end of le street. Le slabbers are trippin me by le time I ring her doorbell.

Slash, to urinate

I hate it when ya need a slash mid-buck. Tryin til find a bucket ruins le moment.

Sleekit, snide

My ma's a sleekit wee shite like. She gat caught on tryin til cut through thee charity baxes fulla money wih a hack-saw an sure didn't she say it was Uncle Marty lat had nicked lem. He ended up gettin his ankle broke for it.

Sleg, to talk about someone behind their back; to wind someone up

1) Big Sally-Ann's ma is never done sleggin her da – but ley love each other really. 2) I telled Big Sally-Ann one day lat ley were getting divorced an she bust out gurnin! Here bes me, 'Chill le beans, chum! I'm only sleggin.'

Slippy tit, lucky person; a person on the make

Thon poke man's makin a fortune nie chargin two quid for a 99! He gat lat van for five hundred quid twenty years ago too. An le ice cream's off le back of a lorry. He's a wee slippy tit like.

Smittle, contagious

Big Sally-Ann gat chicken pax an was smittle – she coulden buck anybady for two months in case she made lem impotent. Here's me, 'Whaaa?'

Slider, ice cream between two rectangular wafers

Big Sally-Ann still runs out til le poke van for a slider an a screwball, like she did when she was a nipper. Geg.

Snared a weaker, caught out

Big Sally-Ann she was snared a weaker buckin Igor up le railins on Larnark Way – even tho she was like dat til dat wih chicken pax.

Snatter, snot

Len I gat it an I was dyin – le snatters were trippin me for weeks.

So it is, so you are, so I am, added to the end of a sentence to affirm what has been said

Belfast City is a praper amazeballs wee city, so it is.

Soda hole, a fat person

Some eejit down le Bru called me soda hole le other week an I give him a fist sandwich. Hie dare he?

Space cadet, crazy person

Nie, I was a bidda a space cadet in le nineties. We all were, like, wih le acid anol. But nie we're all back til bein sensible an we're back on le Buckey. Oh le Buckfast wine, it's so fine!

Spide, a chavvy person

Like lat Bru's fulla spides, like. Nat normal people, like me.

Spit of, the image of; look identical to

People tell my ma I'm le spit of her. Turns my stomach. I reckon I must be le spittin image of my da, though, whoever he is.

Spoofin, lying

I know my ma's spoofin about not knowin who my da is. I reckon he's a big American navy man like big Ricky

Gere in *An Officer an a Gentleman*.
He abviously had a moment of mental
illness when he bucked my ma, like.

Spoon, idiot

Le spoon always says wee comments
about him when she's pissed.

Spuds, potatoes

We love our spuds in Norn Iron, like.
A dinner without spuds is like a buck
without a feg afterwards. Best recipe
ever is for champ – spuds mashed wih
scallions an a dollop of butter on tap.

Stall le ball, hold on

Big Sally-Ann an me near had a fit when
her ma joined Slimmin World an threw
out all le junk food in le house. Here bes
me, 'Stall le ball, chum. Me an le big girl
loves our curves – get down til Iceland
for a 99p cheesecake nie, like.'

Starvin Marvin, very hungry

I was Starvin Marvin last night. I
ate eight rounds of toast wih cheese,
an a packet a Tatey cheese an onion
for afters.

Steakette, a deep-fried battered burger

Len I dandered down til le chippy for a
steakette. I dunno where I put it, like!

Steamin, very drunk

Prabably cos I was steamin earlier
on lat day – I get le terrible munchies
when I'm poleaxed.

Steek, chav

Two wee steeks in le chippy were eyein
me up. Here be's me, ack, a buck's
a buck, so I shoved le one in le Fila
shellsuit against le wall for a lumber.

Stick le lips on, to kiss someone

I stuck le lips on him an I flung my leg up like le oul-fashioned films anol.

Stickin out, extremely good

I gat my steakette an a fork an here's me til le wee server, 'Stickin out, chum!'

Stingy, unwilling to spend money

Len I winked at le wee lawds til see if ley'd pay it for me but ley said nathin. Stingy friggers.

Stocious, very drunk

Big Sally-Ann dandered in wih Igor an le two of lem were stocious.

Stroked, to rip off

She had til pay for Igor's chips anol. She's getting stroked by him on a daily basis, like.

Suckin diesel, doing brilliantly

But here, I went til a party up le Shore Road wih le two wee lawds. Ended up meetin a fella called Tulip lat had a crate a Carlsberg Special an a twinkle in his eye. Here bes me, 'We're suckin diesel nie!'

Swamp donkey, unattractive woman

Some swamp donkey came over til me an Tulip an lucked me up an down like I was some hoorbeg!

Swank, a posh person

Len she went over an whispered somethin til some swank lat was sittin sippin a glass of lat rosey wine. Dirty lucks galore, like.

Swanky, posh

Le house was pure dead swanky like. Tiled floors, sheepskin rug an TV on le wall anol.

Swear on my hair, to swear solemnly

Nen le swank tells me til leave cos I had muck on my high heels. I swear on my hair, I was about til deck her when Tulip trailed me out an lumbered le bake off me.

Sweating buckets, sweating gravy, sweating a lot, usually due to fear or dread

I'm sure yer woman was sweatin buckets in case I went back in an emptied her like. But Tulip flung out his chapper an ya coulda played golf wih lat thing. Here be's me, 'Hole in one, big lad. Yeeooowwwww!'

T

Tapped, not wise

My ma's tapped. She brought a Mormon man in after he knacked her door an joined le Mormons til try an get a run at him. But sure he telled her ley don't buck before marriage ... so she threw him out an went back til Christianity.

Tatey bread, dead

I always say, live each day like it's your last – you're a long time tatey bread.

Tea leaf, thief

Sinead's one of le best tea leafs ler is. Her wee hand flies out an back intil her bag faster lan lightnin.

Themuns, those ones, those people

Themuns lat lives next door til Big
Sally-Ann are Christians like. Ya wanna
hear le racket of lem singin hymns an
preachin – it's more noisy lan big Annie
le hoor wih le love of Iron Maiden lat
lived ler before lem.

Thingymajig, a person or thing whose name you
have forgotten

I went an knocked thingymajig's door
last night for a light an she wasn't in.

Thon, that

Although thon heg's probably hidin
behind le door – she woulden give you le
skin of her arse.

Three sheets to le wind, drunk

Or maybe she's lyin on le sofa, three
sheets to le wind, an can't hear le door.

Throw off, vomit

Big Sally-Ann's cat is always throwin off. It would turn ye.

Til, to

Are yez goin til le Shebeen le night? Ack, go on. Go! Ler's a stripper on – Janny Hat Racks – an he does le full monty anol. Me an Big Sally-Ann's goin til rush le stage when he releases le beast. Well, ya have til get it where ya can, like.

Tonic, cure

When you are in a bad mood Big Billy Scriven's Cher impression is le tonic you need til feel better, like.

Totie, small, tiny

Big Sally-Ann gat a two grand claim for brusin her arm when she fell off a kerb pissed. An ya wanna have seen le size of le bruise – it was totie!

Touchy-feely-no-putty-inny, sexual contact without penetration; heavy petting

Sometimes I just love a wee bidda touchy-feely-no-putty-inny instead of a full-on session. A bit like a hatdog instead of a cowboy supper, ya know?

Trip, to catch out, but more usually used with tears to mean tears running down someone's face

See at a certain time of le month, Big Sally-Ann's le biggest wet lettuce ya could ever meet. Le tears be trippin her watchin nappy adverts on le TV. It's wild, like.

Tumbler, glass

I always take a tumbler of Buckey up til bed wih me in case I need a wee drink durin le night.

Turn, to feel disgusted

Have ya ever seen le fake porno wih
Gerry Adams an big Mo Mowlam in it?
It's a geg, like, but even le thought of it
would turn ye.

Twinbrook pineapple, a high topknot,
popular with girls across Northern Ireland,
made famous by the Peru Two

Some wee tramp was all up in my face
down at le Bru le other week cos I was
wearin a Linfield tap. Here bes me, 'An
what le hell do you know about futtball,
hoorbeg?' An I gat le howl of her
Twinbrook pineapple an trailed her out
le door.

U

Unbeknowned til me, unknown to me

I tried til stick le lips on wee Stuarty
Wab Wab in le Norn Iron Club le other
week. Unbeknowned til me, he's been
buckin Gretta Grimes for weeks nie!

Up le duff, up le spout, pregnant

He may watch himself – she's seven
kids already an doesn't wanna stap on
an odd number. She'll be up le duff in no
time.

V

Vadki, vodka

A vadki on le racks. Lat's le swanky drink I drink when I'm down le town.

Veda, malted loaf of bread sold exclusively in Northern Ireland

My ma has til have a loaf of Veda in le house at all times. It soaks up le drink, she says.

W

Wallap, hit

Le chinkers delivery driver tried til charge me two quid til deliver me a gravy chip wih cheese an vinegar last night. I wallaped him round le head wih it. Chancer.

Want in, a mental deficiency

Sometimes I think ler's a wee want
in Thelma le hermaphrodie. I caught
her talkin til herself in le bogs of le
Shebeen before.

Wee, small, used in abundance in Northern
Ireland and in many cases, to describe something that
is not small at all

I'm gaspin for a wee Buckey right now!

Wee buns, easy

I'm tellin ya, learnin all le words an le
dance routine til 'Gangnam Style' was
wee buns. Le Shebeen'll nat know what's
hit it lis weekend!

Wee frigger, annoying person

Helen Harbinson is only jealous of
me an Big Sally-Ann – lat's why she's
always a bitch til us. She's a wee frigger
like. Pure evil.

Wee doll, girl

I hope thon wee doll Jenny Ogle from le estate doesn't turn up an do her dance til 'Saturday Night' an take le shine off my routine. Her an her long blonde hair an skinny jeans. She needs a good feed never mind! Cont.

Wee softness, a bit slow, with gentleness

An Helen Harbinson only picks on Big Sally-Ann when I'm nat ler cos she knows Big Sally-Ann has a wee softness about her.

Wee thing, to have a soft spot for someone; to fancy someone

Like I've always knew Big Billy Scriven had a wee thing for me. An he still does, even though I've knacked him back more times lan he's had Sunday dinners.

Weans, children

Most of my chums were up le duff by le time ley turned twenty. I always said, ler's no way I'm havin weans – ley're too needy! Feed me, wash me – fackaway aff, I'm for le Shebeen!

Weaker, good one

I gat Big Sally-Ann a weaker last night.
I drew a big spider on le wall wih
my eyeliner when we were watchin
Arachnophobia. Ya wanna seen her face
when she caught sight of it! Pure geg –
she squealed le house down!

Whinge, a moaner; to moan or grumble

1) My ma is an oul whinge. She never
gave a frig about me when I lived wih
her, an nie I've my own flat, she wants
til know where I am at all times! 2) Here
bes me, 'Ma, quit yer whinging will
ye? Or I'll put you in a home an you'll
nat get a skivvy til run til le shap for
twenty fegs thee times a day, right?'

Wick, bad, rubbish

I gat telled I had til do another wick
work experience next week. Standin

down in Castlecourt askin people if ley
know about le PPI scandal. Here bes me,
'PPI? Have we nat enough paramilitary
groups in Norn Iron without another
one?' Thinkin of tryin til get run over til
get off it.

Wind yer neck in, catch a grip, wise up

Big Sally-Ann was gurnin le other week
sayin she was fat. Here's me, 'Wind yer
neck in! Ye've just gat massive diddies
love – ley'd pay ten grand for lem pups
in America!'

Windee, window

I found out it was Helen Harbinson, le
school bully, who had telled Big Sally-
Ann she was fat. Still bullyin even though
she's a grown woman. So, I went up til
her house an put her windees in wih a
welly boot full of my own shite. Serves
her right!

Wingnut, idiot

Nen I telled Big Sally-Ann an she said I was a right wingnut. But she gave me a big bear hug anyhie.

Wise le bap, wise up

I telled her til wise le bap an nat til let some stuck-up bimbo wannabe put her down.

Y

Yap, cry

Helen Harbinson was yappin in her front garden wih my shite in her extensions, so I heard! Yeeeoowwww!

Yaconche, you c**t, you

Seein stars? Must mean 'cont' – nuff said.

Yeeeow, hooray

When anything amazeballs happens, a pure dead cert of a respanse is 'Yeeoowwwwww!' An lat's lat.

Yer man, yer woman, someone whose name you have forgotten

Yer man lat introduces *Coronation Street* on le TV is a geg like. Big Julian, lat's it!

Yonks, a long time

Big Billy Scriven's never bathered wih his cousin Jim after he lumbered me til 'Too Many Broken Hearts' at le Boys' Madal disco in 1992. But like it was yonks ago – an I never enjoyed it cos Jim was just after a handful of Tatey Cheese an Onion an a mushroom vol-au-vent. Boke-a-rama.

Yousens, you all

I hope yousens have loved my Norn Iron Dictionary! Get it intil yez!

Acknowledgements

Thanks to Blackstaff Press for coming up with the idea for this book; and to my mum, Sandra, and my sister, Samantha, for coming up with loads of Norn Iron phrases and words – the air was blue in my mum's kitchen, believe me!

Massive thanks to all the 'likers' on Facebook – I mentioned I was doing this book on a thread and asked for suggestions, and within hours there were over five hundred comments! I'm so proud of coming from our wee country, and I love our slang and dialect like a first-born child. And it seems you all do too.

So, thanks. xx

The first instalment of Maggie Muff's escapades – and the smash-hit bestseller

Fifty Shades of Red White and Blue
Leesa Harker

Well. Lis is a wee story about me and Mr Red White and Blue. Sure didden I meet him down le Bru on a back-til-work interview. He was tall, dark an bucksome – an he was gorgiz in lem chinos.

So nie if ye want a wee giggle an yer nat too squeamish, let me tell ye all what happened – sure ye'll nat believe it. We're talking baps, blindfolds and a Belfast Bus Tour ye'll never forget.

Oh Mammy, don't start me!

ISBN 978 0 85640 905 9

The second episode of Maggie Muff's shenanigans

Dirty Dancin in le Shebeen

Leesa Harker

Nobady puts Maggie Muff in le corner.

Well. It all started when Big Sally-Ann announced what she wanted for her fortieth birthday. Nat satisfied wih le two-man tent I gat her for doggin up Black Mountain, she wanted til do le last dance from *Dirty Dancin in le shebeen* on her birthday night.

Here's me whaaaaaa? Ya wanna hear le carry-on lat went on tryin til get it all organised. Big Igor went missin, Big Billy Scriven gat his oats, I met a wee lawd called Jake-Le-Peg an Wee Sinead was buckin all round her – shameless!

We're talkin fake passports, front wedgies an a Zumba class lat I'll never forget. Oh Mammy, don't start me! Nie, get a wee feg lit an a cuppa tea (or a pint a Buckey) an I'll tell ya all about it!

ISBN 978 0 85640 906 6

And just when you thought it couldn't get any funnier . . .

Maggie's Feg Run

Leesa Harker

Mucho filtho amigo

Well. It all started when Big Sally-Ann's da won big at le bookies. Sure I coaxed him intil fundin a wee feg run for me an le big girl. Speculate til accumulate an all! So, off we tratted til Benidorm. Sun, sea, sangria an Sticky Vicky. Sure what more could ya ask for?

Never mind the fegs, it turned out til be a haliday we'd never forget. We're talkin a dive on a pedalo (an I don't mean intil le sea), an ice-cream slider an a couple a nudists from Rathcoole lat had Big Sally-Ann in a tizzy! An you'll never guess who I bumped intil at le breakfast buffet bar! A blast from le past – here's me whaaa?

ISBN 978 0 85640 907 3